Problem Solving
Grades 4–5
by Becky Daniel-White

Activities Support These Learning Outcomes

Number Sense and Operations
- Understand place value, equivalencies, and representations of whole numbers, fractions, and decimals
- Understand the meanings and properties of operations
- Develop strategies for accurate methods of computation and estimation

Algebra
- Model mathematical situations with graphs, tables, and equations

Data Analysis and Probability
- Collect, organize, and represent data using observations, surveys, tables, and graphs
- Analyze data using measures of mean, median, and mode
- Understand probability as a measure of likelihood and evaluate data to quantify likelihood

Problem Solving
- Develop a variety of problem-solving strategies

Carson-Dellosa Publishing Company, Inc.
Greensboro, North Carolina

Credits

Editor:
Amy Gamble

Layout Design & Art Coordination:
Jon Nawrocik

Inside Illustrations:
Jim Nuttle

Cover Design:
Peggy Jackson

ISBN 0-88724-180-8

Table Of Contents

Chapter I—Addition, Subtraction, Multiplication, and Division

Chapter II— Decimals, Fractions, and Percents

Chapter III—Probability, Statistics, and Logic

To the Teacher

Problem solving is an unique kind of mathematics that requires special processing—processing beyond regular math facts and operations. When solving logic and word problems, the learner must be able to read with comprehension, reason, and communicate solutions.

In the first step—reading—the students must comprehend the story facts and the questions. Students cannot think logically or solve a problem if they do not understand what is being asked. Often, drawing pictures can help children organize and consolidate data. Being able to look at given information in an organized fashion aids students in thinking through a problem and communicating their answers.

In the second step—reasoning—students must understand what steps are needed to take in order to arrive at the solution. To do this, students need a good mathematical vocabulary including terms such as *sum, difference, product,* and *quotient.* Drawing pictures helps students organize their own reasoning steps. Allowing ample opportunities for students to apply reasoning skills and explain their thinking will increase students' ability to problem solve. One way to do this is to challenge students with relevant questions throughout the day. For example: *Lunch is in 50 minutes. Your math page has 10 problems. In order to finish before lunch, approximately how much time can you spend on each problem?* Real-world contexts provide opportunities for students to connect what they are learning to their own world.

Finally—communicating—is essential in problem solving. When students are encouraged to put forth their own ideas and have opportunities to explain and examine them, they learn not only how to reason, but how to communicate ideas to others. In classrooms where problem solving is emphasized, students learn to engage in reasoning and have the opportunity to clearly communicate their thinking processes. Teaching good communication skills is accomplished by making students responsible in two ways: students must articulate their own reasoning and must listen carefully so that they can understand the reasoning of others.

Ways to extend the problem solving activities in this book:

1. Have students create new word problems using the facts in a story. Then, have students exchange papers and solve each other's problems.

2. Change the numbers in a story, and have students rework problems using the new numbers. For example: Double the numbers. Discuss how doubling numbers changes the answers when adding, subtracting, multiplying, and dividing.

3. Have students take turns illustrating a problem on the chalkboard. Encourage other students to guess which problem is being illustrated and/or verbalize the other student's thinking process at each stage.

4. If a student draws a picture to illustrate a problem, ask her to illustrate the same problem in a different way.

5. After students solve a problem, have them list the steps in their reasoning processes.

6. Provide time for students to communicate their thinking processes to each other. Let students share drawings and writing in small groups, and see how many of them used the same reasoning steps. Encourage a variety of ways to find solutions to the same problem.

7. When appropriate, ask students to change the term *sum* to *difference* or *product* to *quotient* and rework a problem. Discuss how changing the operation alters the outcome of the problem.

Animal Longevity

Addition
Series of 1– and 2–Digit Numbers

Directions

Carefully read each question and decide what is being asked. Write an equation for each problem along with your complete answer.

The Story: Animals can be expected to live a certain numbers of years—this is called average longevity. Some animals live longer than the average, or to a maximum longevity. The average and maximum longevity of eleven animals is shown below.

	camel	cow	elephant	hippo	lion
Average:	12 years	15 years	40 years	41 years	15 years
Maximum:	50 years	30 years	77 years	54 years	30 years

	mouse	pig	rhinoceros	sheep	zebra	giraffe
Average:	3 years	10 years	20 years	12 years	15 years	10 years
Maximum:	6 years	27 years	50 years	20 years	50 years	33 years

1. Find the total years lived by the average hippo, rhinoceros, lion, and zebra.

2. What is the total of the maximum longevity of a cow, pig, sheep, and mouse?

3. The total years lived by the average zebra, lion, camel, and giraffe is what?

4. Altogether, what is the maximum number of years that a lion, zebra, pig, and mouse can live?

5. What is the sum of the years lived by an average lion, zebra, pig, and mouse?

6. Altogether, what is the number of years the average mouse, pig, lion, and sheep can be expected to live?

7. Find the total maximum longevity of animals on the chart that sometimes live fifty years or more.

Name _____ Date _____

Average Airborne Speeds

Directions

Carefully read each question and decide what is being asked. Using the average speed of each aircraft, write an equation for each problem along with your complete answer.

The Story: The Air Transportation Association figures the average airborne speed for common aircraft models. Use the table to solve the problems.

Model	Avg. Speed	Model	Avg. Speed
B747-400	538 mph	B474-100	521 mph
B474-200/300	535 mph	B777	512 mph
DC-10-40	506 mph	L-1011-100/200	490 mph
DC-10-10	503 mph	DC-10-30	523 mph
A300-600	468 mph	MD-11	526 mph
L-1011-500	524 mph	B767-300ER	496 mph
B757-200	465 mph	B767-200ER	487 mph
A310-300	498 mph		

1. Altogether, how many miles can a B747-400 and DC-10-40 fly in one hour?

2. What is the sum of miles that can be traveled in an hour by an A310-300 and a B757-200?

3. Find the total number of miles traveled in an hour by a B474-100, B777, and a DC-10-10.

4. The B474-200/300, A310-300, and MD-11 travel a total of how many miles in an hour?

5. In an hour, what is the total miles traveled by a B767-300ER, B757-200, and B767-200ER?

6. The DC-10-30, DC-10-10, and A300-600 can travel a total of how many miles in one hour?

7. Find the total miles traveled in an hour by the L-1011-100/200, L-1011-500, and MD-11.

Paperback Book Club

Subtraction

2-Digit Numbers

Directions

Carefully read each question and decide what is being asked. Write an equation for each problem along with your complete answer.

The Story: The paperback book club has eight official members. The table shows how many mystery, biography, and fantasy paperbacks each member has. Use the table to help you solve the problems.

Member	Mystery	Biography	Fantasy
Milo	88	56	10
Joshua	35	91	59
Naomi	28	17	66
Denzel	47	81	33
Colin	49	32	63
Coco	55	67	79
Iris	93	58	22
Malcolm	78	33	41

1. How many more mystery paperback books does Iris have than Naomi?

2. What is the difference between the biography collections of Denzel and Milo?

3. Find the difference between Malcolm's mystery collection and Joshua's fantasy collection.

4. The difference between Colin's fantasy collection and Iris's biography collection is what?

5. How many more paperback biographies does Coco have than Iris?

6. What is the difference between the top biography collection and the top fantasy collection?

7. What is the difference between Malcolm's fantasy collection and Joshua's mystery collection?

Name _____ Date _____

The Years of Invention

Directions

Carefully read each question and decide what is being asked. Write an equation for each problem along with your complete answer.

The Story: It's hard to imagine what life was like before frozen food and microwaves. Some of the dates of inventions might surprise you. Use the table to solve the problems.

Invention	Year	Invention	Year
Adding machine	1642	Kaleidoscope	1817
Aerosol spray	1926	Incandescent lamp	1879
Airplane motor	1903	Electric locomotive	1851
Automobile gasoline	1889	Microphone	1877
Balloons	1783	Motorcycle	1885
Modern bicycle	1885	Talking movie	1927
Modern camera	1888	Lawn mower	1831
Floppy disk	1970	Nylon	1937
Frozen food	1924	Paper	105
Helicopter	1939	Parachute	1785
Ice-making machine	1851	Ballpoint pen	1888

1. How many years older is the invention of the ice-making machine than the incandescent lamp?

2. How many more years old are balloons than kaleidoscopes?

3. How many years passed between the invention of paper and floppy disks?

4. After parachutes were invented, how many years went by before the airplane motor was invented?

5. What is the difference in years between the invention of ballpoint pens and nylon?

6. Adding machines are how much older than modern cameras?

7. After modern bicycles were invented, how many years passed before people could ride their bikes to see a talking movie?

Donating Desserts

Add & Subtract
1– and 2–Digit Numbers

Directions

Finish the chart. Then, carefully read each question and decide what is being asked. Write the equations needed to solve each problem along with your complete answer.

The Story: Olivia's club baked desserts for the homeless shelter. Olivia made a dozen of each dessert. Becca made 10 brownies, 12 cupcakes, 24 cookies, and 8 tarts. Kira made 24 brownies, 6 cupcakes, 30 cookies, and 12 tarts. Emily made 8 brownies, 20 cupcakes, 36 cookies, and 6 tarts. Marta made 8 brownies, 8 cupcakes, 36 cookies, and no tarts.

	brownies	cupcakes	cookies	tarts
Olivia	12	12	12	12
Becca				
Kira				
Emily				
Marta				

1. Did the girls bake more brownies or cupcakes?

2. What is the difference between the total number of cookies and tarts baked?

3. Did the girls bake more cupcakes or cookies?

4. Find the difference between the total desserts baked by Becca and Olivia.

5. The difference between the total desserts baked by Kira and Emily is what?

6. What is the difference between the top baker's total and Becca's total?

7. The difference between the top baker's total and Marta's total is what?

Name _____ Date _____

Science Quizzes

Add & Subtract
2- and 3-Digit Numbers

Directions

Finish the chart. Then, carefully read each question and decide what is being asked. Write the equations needed to solve each problem along with your complete answer.

The Story: Mrs. Lamb gave a science quiz every Friday in February. Javon's scores were (in points) 99, 100, 85, and 80. Sarah's scores were 90, 88, 100, and 87. Ryan's scores were 66, 77, 69, and 100. Tamika's scores were 83, 90, 99, and 77. Jake's scores were 97, 93, 90, and 91. Erin's scores were 100, 99, 100, and 98.

	#1	#2	#3	#4	Total
Javon	99	100	85	80	364
Sarah					
Ryan					
Tamika					
Jake					
Erin					

1. How much higher was Sarah's total score than Javon's?

2. What was the difference between Jake's scores on the first and second Fridays compared to his scores on the third and fourth Fridays?

3. Find the difference between Erin's scores on the second and third Fridays compared to her scores on the first and fourth Fridays.

4. What is the difference between Erin's and Jake's totals?

5. Javon's total score was how much higher than Ryan's?

6. How much higher was Tamika's total score than Ryan's?

7. Jake's total score was how much higher than Sarah's?

Name _____ Date _____

Top Movies

Directions

Carefully read each question and decide what is being asked. Write an equation for each problem along with your complete answer. Write the full amount for each answer and remember to include the dollar sign. For example: 36 would be written as $36,000,000.

The Story:
The table lists the box-office gross of movies in the U.S. and Canada.

Movie Title	Gross in Millions of Dollars
Got Sam	68
Courageous Molly	67
Jungle Juice	54
Mother of the Groom	50
Monkey in the House	40
The Cowboy in the Basement	36
Smart and Clever	68
Baby Face	57
The Telephone Caper	50
The Brave Bunch	47
Mighty Mississippi Mom	38
A Good Movie	35

1. If *Got Sam* had grossed three times the amount it did, how many dollars would the movie have earned?

2. If *Baby Face* had grossed as much in each of the countries France, Italy, and Spain as it did in the U.S. and Canada, how much would it have grossed in the three European countries?

3. If *Monkey in the House* had been shown eight times as long, how much could the movie have grossed?

4. If *Courageous Molly* had earned six times as much as it did, what would the movie's total gross have been?

5. If *Mother of the Groom* had played four times as long as it did, altogether how much could the movie have grossed?

6. How much could *Mighty Mississippi Mom* have grossed if it had played eight times longer?

7. If the lowest grossing movie had grossed three times as much as it did, how much would it have grossed?

Name _____ Date _____

Recycling Classrooms

Directions

Carefully read each question and decide what is being asked. Write an equation for each problem along with your complete answer.

The Story: To earn money for charity, three classrooms spent a school week (5 days) gathering recyclables: newspapers, glass bottles, and cardboard boxes.

	Newspapers	Glass bottles	Cardboard boxes
Mr. Ella's class	610	622	589
Mrs. Janelle's class	510	521	489
Ms. Reneé's class	701	713	677

1. If Mr. Ella's class and Mrs. Janelle's class had collected the same number of newspapers each week for 12 weeks, how many newspapers would the classes have collected in all?

2. If Mrs. Janelle's class and Ms. Reneé's class collect glass bottles for 25 days at the same rate they did the first week, how many bottles can the students collect?

3. If Ms. Reneé's and Mr. Ella's classes collect cardboard boxes at the same rate they did the first week, how many boxes could they collect altogether in 15 weeks?

4. Find the number of glass bottles that all three classes, if they worked at their same rates, could collect in 15 weeks.

5. If the classes collected at their same rates for 17 weeks, what would be the sum of newspapers they could have collected?

6. Working at their same rates, Mrs. Janelle's and Ms. Reneé's classes could have collected how many newspapers in 90 days?

7. In one week, how much money could the classes have earned for charity if they were paid a nickel for each item collected?

Baseball Card Collectors

Division

3–Digit Numbers by 1–Digit Numbers

Directions

Carefully read each question and decide what is being asked. Write an equation for each problem along with your complete answer.

The Story: Seven friends collect baseball cards. José has 702 cards, Kevin has 616 cards, Nathan has 546 cards, Aaron has 699 cards, Caleb has 293 cards, Hunter has 508 cards, and Thomas has 846 cards.

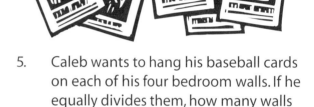

1. If José divides his cards into eight equal stacks, how many cards will there be in each stack? Will there be any cards left over?

2. Kevin wants to divide his cards into equal stacks—one stack for each day of the week. Can this be done?

3. Eight equal stacks of Nathan's cards will each contain how many cards with how many cards left over?

4. Aaron wants to put his cards into an album. If each page holds six cards, how many pages will he need?

5. Caleb wants to hang his baseball cards on each of his four bedroom walls. If he equally divides them, how many walls will have an extra card?

6. If Hunter equally divides his baseball cards into nine piles, how many cards will be in each pile? How many cards will be left over?

7. If Thomas divides his cards equally between himself and eight friends and gives the remaining cards to his sister, how many baseball cards will each boy get? How many cards will his sister get?

The Little Theater

Directions

Carefully read each question and decide what is being asked. Write an equation for each problem along with your complete answer.

The Story: The Little Theater has live productions. It charges different prices for different shows. All of the tickets for one show cost the same.

1. On Saturday night, the total made from the ticket sales at the Little Theater was $132. Forty-four tickets were sold. How much did each ticket cost?

2. If 73 people paid a total of $365 to see Sunday's matinee, how much did each ticket cost?

5. The total earned by the theater on New Year's Day was $637. Ninety-one people each spent how much for a ticket?

3. On Christmas Day, the Little Theater featured The Nutcracker ballet. They sold 84 tickets and took in $336. How much did each person pay for a ticket?

6. If the total for 55 people to come to a midnight show was $330, how much was each ticket?

7. A dinner musical earned the Little Theater $828. If 92 people came to the dinner show, how much did each ticket cost?

4. A live performance by a comedian earned the theater $536. How much did each of the 67 people pay to see the comedian?

Name _____ Date _____

The Reading Club

Directions

Carefully read each question and decide what is being asked. Write an equation for each problem along with your complete answer.

The Story: The students in the after-school reading club keep weekly reading logs of the number of pages they read each day. Use the table to solve the problems.

	Monday	Tuesday	Wednesday	Thursday	Friday
Bria	80	0	144	60	90
Jon	220	180	0	23	89
Lulu	144	67	99	10	150
Amos	68	120	0	99	87

1. What is the sum of pages read by Bria on Monday and Friday?

2. What is the difference between the number of pages read by Jon on Monday and Tuesday?

3. Find the product of the pages Amos read on Tuesday and Wednesday.

4. If Amos read for four hours on Tuesday, what was the average number of pages that he read each hour?

5. Lulu read for five hours on Friday. Find the quotient to show the number of pages that she read each hour.

6. What is the sum of the pages read by all four students on Wednesday?

7. What is Lulu's average number of pages read in a day this week?

Name _____   Date _____

The Paper Boys

Mixed Practice

Choosing an Operation

Directions

Carefully read each question and decide what is being asked. Write the equations needed to solve each problem along with your complete answer.

The Story: Connor, Mikah, and Isaac have paper routes. They deliver papers six days a week. Connor has 45 customers on his route. Mikah has 59 customers on his route. Isaac has the longest route of all—111 customers.

1. How many more papers does Isaac deliver in one week than Connor?

2. Isaac delivered 1,332 papers. How many weeks did it take him?

3. Each week, how many more papers does Mikah deliver than Connor?

4. Mikah delivered 1,770 papers. How many weeks did it take him to deliver that many papers?

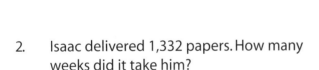

5. How many more papers does Isaac deliver each week than Mikah?

6. Connor delivered 540 papers. How many weeks did it take him to deliver that many papers?

7. Each week, what is the total number of papers delivered by all three boys?

Shaping Up

Directions

Carefully read each question and decide what is being asked. Write the equations needed to solve each problem along with your complete answer.

The Story: Three friends, Kayla, Seth, and Lucas, are faithful joggers. Each weekday, Kayla jogs for 30 minutes. Seth jogs for 20 minutes every day, including the weekends. Lucas jogs for 15 minutes each weekday and an hour on Saturday mornings.

1. How many more minutes each week does Kayla jog than Lucas?

2. Each week Seth jogs how many more minutes than Lucas?

3. How many weeks does it take Kayla to jog for a total of five hours?

4. In four weeks, how many minutes does Lucas spend jogging?

5. If Kayla kept her jogging schedule every week, except two vacation weeks, how many hours will she jog in one year?

6. In four weeks, how many more minutes does Kayla spend jogging than Seth?

7. Each week, do the three friends spend more or less than eight hours jogging altogether?

Come Seven or Eleven

Mixed Practice

Culminating Game

Object of the Game: Get the highest possible score in ten rolls of three dice.

Materials Needed: Paper, pencil, three dice

Directions:

1. Number a sheet of paper from one to ten.
2. Roll three dice.
3. Using all three numbers (or digits) indicated by the dice, the player tries to make an equation with an answer of seven or eleven.
4. Digits may be added, subtracted, multiplied, divided, or combined into two-digit numbers.
5. If a seven is made, the player gets a score of 7 points. If eleven is made, the player gets a score of 11 points. If seven or eleven cannot be made, the player scores 0 points.
6. Play nine more rounds.
7. Check the scoreboard to see how well you did.

Competition:

If playing against other players, take turns rolling the dice. Play ten rounds. The person with the highest total is declared the winner.

Sample Game:

Roll one—6, 1, 1 — $6 + 1 = 7$; $7 \times 1 = 7$ (Score 7 points—total 7)
Roll two—1, 3, 5 — $5 + 3 = 8$; $8 - 1 = 7$ (Score 7 points—total 14)
Roll three—2, 3, 6 — $2 + 3 + 6 = 11$ (Score 11 points—total 25)
Roll four— 3, 5, 5 — $5 + 5 = 10$; $10 - 3 = 7$ (Score 7 points—total 32)
Roll five—1, 3, 6 — $13 - 6 = 7$ (Score 7 points—total 39)
Roll six—4, 7, 9 — $49 \div 7 = 7$ (Score 7 points—total 46)
Roll seven—3, 5, 5 — $35 \div 5 = 7$ (Score 7 points—total 53)
Roll eight—1, 6, 7 — $17 - 6 = 11$ (Score 11 points—total 64)
Roll nine—2, 2, 2 — $22 \div 2 = 11$ (Score 11 points—total 75)
Roll ten— 3, 4, 5 — $3 \times 4 = 12$; $12 - 5 = 7$ (Score 7 points—game total 82)

Scoreboard:

A score over 90 is extraordinary!
A score of 89–70 is excellent.
A score of 69–50 is good.
A score of 49–30 is okay.
A score of 29–0 is the pits. Try again.
Play as many games as it takes until you get an extraordinary game—go for the gold!

United States Car Sales

Decimals

Addition

Directions

Carefully read each question and decide what is being asked. Write an equation for each problem along with your complete answer.

The Story: The American Automobile Manufacturers Association tracks U.S. car sales. The chart below shows the percent of cars sold according to sizes: small, midsize, large, and luxury. Use the chart to solve the problems.

Year	Small	Midsize	Large	Luxury
1990	32.8%	44.8%	9.4%	13.0%
1991	33.0%	44.9%	8.2%	13.9%
1992	32.9%	44.5%	9.2%	13.4%
1993	32.8%	43.3%	11.1%	12.8%
1994	29.2%	45.6%	11.7%	13.5%
1995	27.1%	48.5%	10.8%	13.6%

1. What percent of cars sold in 1995 were either large or luxury?

2. In 1994, what percent of cars sold were either small or midsize?

5. In 1991, the percent of cars sold that were either small, midsize, large, or luxury was what?

3. The total percent of midsize and large cars sold in 1990 was what?

6. In 1994, what percent of cars sold were either small or luxury?

4. Find the percent of midsize, large, and luxury cars sold in 1992.

7. In which year were the sales of midsize, large, and luxury cars 67% of cars sold?

Olympic Hurdles

Decimals

Subtraction

Directions

Carefully read each question and decide what is being asked. Write an equation for each problem along with your complete answer.

The Story: The 400-meter hurdles is an Olympic event. The table shows the winning times in that event over a forty-year period. Use the table to solve the problems.

Year	Gold Winner	Record Set
1996	Derrick Adkins, U. S.	47.54 seconds
1992	Kevin Young, U. S.	46.78 seconds
1988	Andre Phillips, U. S.	47.19 seconds
1984	Edwin Moses, U. S.	47.75 seconds
1980	Volker Beck, E. Germany	48.7 seconds
1976	Edwin Moses, U. S.	47.64 seconds
1972	John Akii-Bua, Uganda	47.82 seconds
1968	Dave Hemery, Great Britain	48.12 seconds
1964	Rex Cawley, U. S.	49.6 seconds
1960	Glenn Davis, U. S.	49.3 seconds
1956	Glenn Davis, U. S.	50.1 seconds

1. How much faster did Dave Hemery complete the 400-meter hurdles than Rex Cawley?

2. In 1960, by how many seconds did Glenn Davis break his 1956 time?

5. Volker Beck's time was how much faster than Dave Hemery's?

3. From 1956 to 1996, how many seconds difference were there in winning times?

6. By how many seconds did Kevin Young beat the previous winning time?

4. In 1984, how many more seconds did it take Edwin Moses to complete the event than in 1976?

7. How much faster did Andre Phillips complete the 400-meter hurdles than John Akii-Bua?

Commuting

Decimals

Multiplication

Directions

Carefully read each question and decide what is being asked. Write an equation for each problem along with your complete answer.

The Story: The teachers at Franklin School each travel a different number of kilometers to get to school. Mr. Dylan drives 20.4 km to the city from his farm. Mrs. Haley drives 18.5 km. Ms. Morgan lives 9.3 km from the school. Mr. Gabriel rides his bike 2.3 km to school. Mr. Logan lives 6.7 km from the school. He only teaches three days a week.

1. What is the number of kilometers traveled back and forth to work each day by Mr. Dylan?

2. Altogether, how many kilometers does Mrs. Haley drive to and from school each week?

3. How many kilometers does Ms. Morgan travel back and forth to school in six weeks?

4. Altogether, how many kilometers does Mr. Gabriel ride his bike to and from school in four weeks?

5. Altogether, how many kilometers does Mr. Logan travel to and from school in four weeks?

6. In 35 school days, how many kilometers does Ms. Morgan travel to and from school?

7. Does Mr. Dylan travel more or less than 200 kilometers back and forth to school each week?

Speedy Beasts

Decimals

Multiple Operations

Directions

Carefully read each question and decide what is being asked. Write the equations needed to solve each problem along with your complete answer.

The Story: A garden snail can travel .03 miles per hour. A lion can run 49.50 miles per hour. An elephant can run 25.30 miles per hour. A zebra can run 40.25 miles per hour.

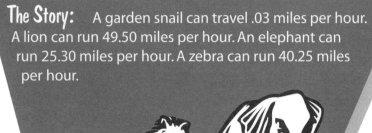

.03 mph   49.50 mph   25.30 mph   40.25 mph

1. How much faster can a lion run than a zebra?

2. A snail crawled two hours one day and four hours the next. Altogether, how far did the snail travel?

3. An elephant traveled three hours one day and one hour the next. Altogether, how many miles did the elephant travel?

4. How many miles can a snail travel in 100 hours?

5. If a zebra can run without getting tired, how many miles will it travel in five hours?

6. How much faster can an elephant run than a snail can crawl?

7. If a snail traveled for five weeks without stopping, could it go as far as an elephant can go in one hour?

Pancake Breakfast

Decimals

Multiple Operations

Directions

Carefully read each question and decide what is being asked. Write the equations needed to solve each problem along with your complete answer.

The Story: The local youth club is raising money by holding a pancake breakfast. Use the menu below to answer the questions.

pancakes (4)	$3.50	pancake platter (4) with sausage	$6.25
pancake (6)	$4.25	pancake platter (6) with sausage	$7.00
pancake (8)	$6.00	pancake platter (8) with sausage	$7.75

orange juice $1.55	side order of bacon $2.15
coffee $0.50	side order of ham $2.85
milk $0.90	scrambled eggs $0.75 each

4. How much more does it cost to buy an 8-pancake platter than eight pancakes without sausage?

1. What will it cost to buy a 4-pancake platter, side order of bacon, orange juice, and coffee?

5. If the profit on a 6-pancake platter is $3.50, how much will the youth club make on twenty of those breakfasts?

2. How much more does it cost to buy a 6-pancake platter than six pancakes without sausage?

6. Six eggs and a side order of ham costs how much?

3. What is the total cost of five 6-pancake platters and five coffees?

7. Eight children ordered the 8-pancake platter, each with milk. What is the total bill?

Mr. Jett's Scout Troop

Percents

Addition & Subtraction

Directions

Carefully read each question and decide what is being asked. Write an equation for each problem along with your complete answer.

The Story: There are ten scouts in Mr. Jett's troop: Jasper, Julian, Miles, Juan, Mark, Paul, Mason, Jared, Evan, and Alex. Each boy represents 10% of the troop.

1. What percent of Mr. Jett's troop has a name beginning with the letter J or E?

2. What percent of Mr. Jett's troop has either a four-letter or six-letter name?

3. Find the percentage of Mr. Jett's troop that has a name that begins or ends with a vowel.

4. What is the percentage of Mr. Jett's troop that has a name beginning with the letter J or M?

5. What is the difference between the percent of the troop with a J name and an M name?

6. What percent of the troop doesn't have the letter A in his name?

7. Find the difference of the percent of boys with four-letter names and five-letter names.

Name _____ Date _____

Spelling Test Scores

Directions

Record each student's score on the chart. Then, carefully read each question and decide what is being asked. Write the equations needed to solve each problem along with your complete answer.

The Story: The spelling test had twenty words. Each correctly spelled word was worth 5%. Trevor didn't miss any words. Jackson missed one word. Angela missed three words. Ysia missed six words. Jade missed nine words. Grades: 100% –95% = A; 90% –80% = B; 70%–60% = C; 50%–40% = D; less than 40% = F

1. What percentage of the words did Ysia miss?

2. Find the difference in the percentage received by Angela and Ysia.

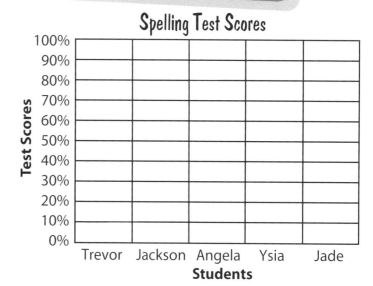

3. What percentage of the words did Jade miss?

4. What percentage of words did Trevor get correct?

5. Altogether, what percentage of words did Ysia and Jade miss?

6. If Angela had gotten two more words correct, what would have been her grade?

7. If Jade took a makeup test and got 18 words correct, by what percent did she improve?

Name _____ Date _____

Mrs. Lion's Animal Club

Directions

Fill in the circle graph and key with the information from the story. Then, carefully read each question and decide what is being asked. Write the equations needed to solve each problem along with your complete answer.

The Story: Mrs. Lion leads an after-school club for animal lovers. There are twenty students in the club. Each section of the circle graph represents one student. 25% of the club likes wild animals best. 20% likes rodents best. 15% favors dogs, and an equal percent favors cats. 10% likes birds, and 5% prefers reptiles.

1. What is the total percent of students who like dogs or cats best?

☐ wild

☐ rodents

☐ dogs

☐ cats

☐ birds

☐ reptiles

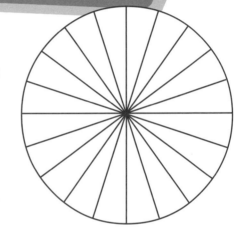

Favorite Animals

2. The sum of students who favor birds, reptiles, or rodents is what percent?

3. The difference between the dog lovers and bird lovers is what percent?

6. Altogether, what percent of the club didn't pick dogs or reptiles as their favorite?

4. What is the percent of students who chose animals other than cats?

7. How many students chose dogs or cats as their favorite animals?

5. Find the total percentage of students that favor either rodents, cats, or reptiles.

Favorite Foods

Like Fractions

Addition & Subtraction

Directions

Color the circle graph and key like this: pizza, red; hamburgers, blue; fried chicken, yellow; shrimp, green; steaks, purple; hot dogs, orange. Then, carefully read each question and decide what is being asked. Use fractions to write the equations needed for each problem along with your complete answer.

The Story: There are 32 students in Mr. Luis's class. When asked about their favorite foods, ten children said pizza. Nine children chose hamburgers. Seven chose fried chicken. Three chose shrimp. Two chose steaks, and only one chose hot dogs.

☐ pizza

☐ hot dogs

☐ steaks

☐ shrimp

☐ hamburgers

☐ fried chicken

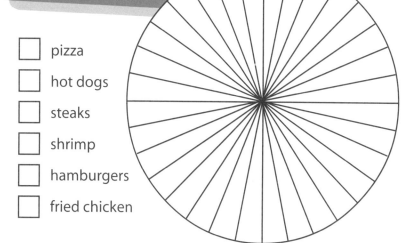

Favorite Foods

1. What is the fractional difference between students who picked pizza or hamburgers and those who chose shrimp or steaks?

2. What is the fractional difference between students who picked pizza or fried chicken versus those who picked shrimp or hot dogs?

5. The group of students that is represented by the fraction $\frac{1}{16}$ chose which food?

3. Which is greater—the fraction of students who chose pizza or those who chose either chicken, shrimp, or hot dogs?

6. The fractional part of the class who chose hamburgers, fried chicken, or shrimp is what?

7. Which is larger, the fractional group who choose fried chicken or the group who chose steak or shrimp?

4. Which fractional group is larger—those who like either hamburgers or shrimp or those who like hot dogs or pizza?

Fractions of September

Like Fractions

Addition & Subtraction

Directions

Carefully read each question and decide what is being asked. Use fractions to write an equation for each problem along with your complete answer. Reduce answers to the lowest terms.

The Story: Use the calendar below to write fractions to answer the questions.

September

Sun.	Mon.	Tues.	Wed.	Thurs.	Fri.	Sat.
			1	2	3	4
5	6	7	8	9	10	11
12	13	14	15	16	17	18
19	20	21	22	23	24	25
26	27	28	29	30		

1. What fractional part of the days in September fall on a Thursday or Friday?

2. What is the fractional part of the days in September that fall on weekends?

3. What fractional part of the dates in September do not have the digit 2 in them?

4. What fractional part of the days in September fall on a Monday, Tuesday, or Wednesday?

5. The days in September that come before the second Friday are represented by what fraction?

6. What is the fractional part of days in September that fall on a Friday, Saturday, or Sunday?

7. What is the fractional difference between the days that fall on Wednesdays and the days that fall on Mondays?

Savannah's Ribbon Shop

Unlike Fractions

Comparing

Directions

Carefully read each question and decide what is being asked. Use <, >, and = signs to write an equation or inequality for each problem. Find a common denominator to help you solve each problem.

The Story: At Savannah's Ribbon Shop, you can buy ribbon by the meter or by fractions of a meter. Use the fraction bars to help you answer the questions.

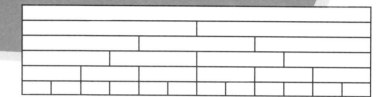

1. Which is longer: $\frac{3}{4}$ meter or $\frac{5}{6}$ meter?

2. How do $\frac{9}{12}$ meter and $\frac{4}{6}$ meter compare?

5. How do $\frac{9}{12}$ meter and $\frac{3}{4}$ meter compare?

3. Which is longer: $\frac{1}{3}$ meter or $\frac{1}{4}$ meter?

6. Is the sum of $\frac{5}{6}$ meter and $\frac{1}{12}$ meter more or less than a whole meter?

4. How do $\frac{1}{2}$ meter and $\frac{1}{3}$ meter compare?

7. Which is longer: $\frac{11}{12}$ meter or $\frac{7}{8}$ meter?

Lulu's Bakery

Directions

Carefully read each question and decide what is being asked. Use <, >, and = signs to write an equation or inequality for each problem. Find a common denominator to help you solve each problem.

The Story: At Lulu's Bakery, the cherry cheesecakes are cut into eight slices. Peach cobblers are cut into six slices.

cherry cheesecake   peach cobbler

1. Zelda ate a piece of cherry cheesecake. Sophia ate a piece of peach cobbler. Which girl ate the most dessert?

2. Simon bought three slices of peach cobbler. Spike bought five pieces of cherry cheesecake. Which boy bought the most dessert?

5. Jason ate a piece of cherry cheesecake, and Noah ate two pieces of peach cobbler. Which dessert had the most left?

3. Jolie ate three slices of cherry cheesecake, and Lauren ate two pieces of peach cobbler. Which girl ate the most dessert?

6. If Brian bought $\frac{1}{2}$ of a cheesecake and Juan bought $\frac{2}{3}$ of a peach cobbler, which pie had the most left?

4. If Jack bought four pieces of cherry cheesecake and Adam bought three pieces of peach cobbler, which boy bought the most dessert?

7. If four pieces of a cherry cheesecake and four slices of a peach cobbler were left, which dessert had the most left?

Emma's Handiwork

Unlike Fractions

Comparing & Adding

Directions

Use the illustration to help you simplify unlike fractions. Carefully read each question and decide what is being asked. Write an equation for each problem. Reduce answers to the lowest terms.

The Story: Emma makes tablecloths, scarves, and hankies. She bought six yards of material and cut each yard into pieces as illustrated with the fraction bars. Color the fraction bars as indicated by each problem.

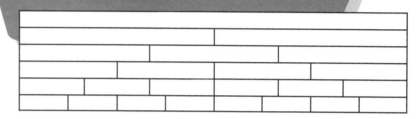

1. Emma used four $\frac{1}{8}$-yard pieces plus two $\frac{1}{6}$-yard pieces to make hankies. Color that much fabric red. Altogether, how much material did she use?

2. Emma sewed together three $\frac{1}{4}$-yard pieces and one $\frac{1}{3}$-yard piece to make a scarf. Color that much fabric blue. How many yards did she use in all for the scarf?

3. Emma sewed together a $\frac{1}{2}$-yard piece and a $\frac{1}{3}$-yard piece to make a scarf. Color that much fabric green. Altogether, how much fabric did Emma use for the scarf?

4. Which takes more fabric to make—three $\frac{1}{6}$-yard hankies or four $\frac{1}{8}$-yard hankies? Color that much fabric yellow.

5. If Emma uses a one-yard piece of fabric to make $\frac{1}{8}$-yard hankies, how many can she make? Color that much fabric purple.

6. Color one $\frac{1}{2}$-yard piece of fabric orange. If Emma wants to make four $\frac{1}{6}$-yard hankies. Is $\frac{1}{2}$ yard enough material?

Name _____ Date _____

Johnny's Cakes

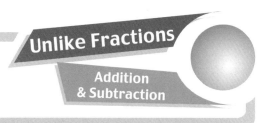

Directions

Carefully read each question and decide what is being asked. Use fractions to write the equations needed to solve each problem along with your complete answer. Reduce answers to the lowest terms.

The Story: For the bake sale, Johnny baked three square cakes. He cut the lemon-coconut cake in half. He cut the milk-chocolate cake into quarters. The strawberries 'n' cream cake, he cut into sixteenths.

lemon-coconut   milk-chocolate   strawberries 'n' cream

1. If Johnny sold Milo five pieces of strawberries 'n' cream cake, what fractional part of the strawberries 'n' cream cake was left?

4. If Johnny sold Colin the last four pieces of strawberries 'n' cream cake, what fractional part of the cake did Colin buy?

2. If Johnny sold Elsa one of the lemon-coconut halves and two pieces of the milk-chocolate cake, what fractional part of a whole cake did Elsa buy?

5. Lila bought a piece of lemon-coconut and three slices of strawberries 'n' cream. What fractional part of a whole cake did Lila buy?

3. What fractional part of a whole cake is one piece of milk-chocolate cake and four pieces of strawberries 'n' cream cake?

6. If before the bake sale, Naomi took a photograph of Johnny holding one piece of each kind of cake, what fractional part of a whole cake was in the photograph?

7. How many pieces of strawberries 'n' cream equals a piece of lemon-coconut?

Carla's Chocolates

Fractions

Multiple Operations

Directions

Carefully read each question and decide what is being asked. Use fractions to write the equations needed to solve each problem along with your complete answer. Reduce answers to lowest terms.

The Story: Carla makes delicious homemade chocolates. All of her friends love to eat them. The milk chocolate bars she cuts into 4 squares. The cherry chocolate bars she cuts into 8 equal triangles. She cuts the dark chocolate bars into 2 triangles. And the peanut cluster bars are cut into 16 chunks.

dark chocolate   **peanut cluster**   **milk chocolate**   **cherry chocolate**

1. If 5 of Carla's friends each ate 2 peanut cluster chunks, what fraction of the peanut cluster bar is left?

2. If 3 of Carla's friends each ate a dark chocolate triangle, how many dark chocolate bars did her friends eat?

3. If Carla divided a peanut cluster bar between 4 friends, how many chunks would each friend get?

4. How many triangles of cherry chocolates equals 2 squares of a milk chocolate bar?

5. If 7 of Carla's friends ate peanut cluster chunks, what fractional part of the peanut cluster bar was left?

6. How many peanut cluster chunks equal the same fraction as 6 cherry chocolate triangles?

7. How many peanut cluster chunks equal the same fraction as one dark chocolate triangle?

Wheel of Fortune

Directions

Carefully read each question and decide what is being asked. Write the equations needed to solve each problem along with your complete answer. Reduce answers to the lowest terms.

The Story: Each section of the wheel represents 5% of the whole, $\frac{1}{20}$ of the whole, and .05 of the whole.

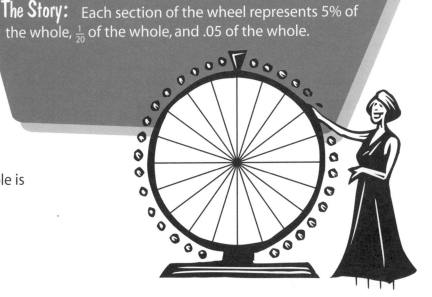

1. What fractional part of the whole is represented by six sections?

2. What is the decimal that represents eight of the sections?

3. Ten of the sections is what percent of the whole wheel?

4. What fractional part of the wheel is represented by twelve sections?

5. How many sections of the wheel are represented by .35?

6. Find the number of sections that represent 45% of the wheel.

7. What fractional part of the wheel is represented by 50% of the sections?

Name _____ Date _____

Dare to Compare

Directions

Carefully read each question and decide what is being asked. Follow the directions for coloring and then write the equations needed to solve each problem along with your complete answer.

The Story: When the whole is divided into 100 parts, each part represents $\frac{1}{100}$, 1%, or .01 of the whole.

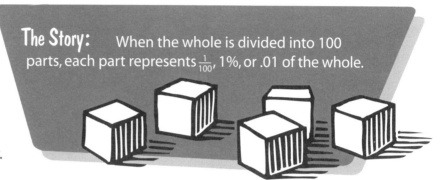

1. Color $\frac{50}{100}$ orange. What decimal and percent is colored?

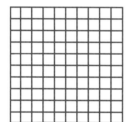

2. Color .08 red. What fractional part of the whole and percent is colored?

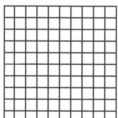

3. Color .80 yellow. What fractional part of the whole and percent is colored?

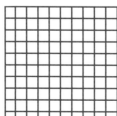

4. Color 35% purple. What fraction and decimal is colored?

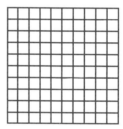

5. Color 75% purple. What decimal and fractional part of the whole is colored?

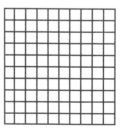

6. Color $\frac{1}{10}$ green. What decimal and percent is colored?

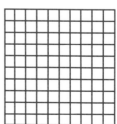

Name _____ Date _____

Race to Seven Hundred

Object of the Game:
Get 700 points in ten rolls of three dice.

Materials Needed:
Paper, pencil, three dice

Directions:
1. Choose one person to keep the answer key.
2. Number a sheet of paper from one to ten.
3. Roll three dice.
4. Choose two of the numbers and make a fraction of one or less than one.
5. If the player can name the percent and decimal represented by the fraction, he gets the number of points indicated by the percentage. If a player cannot name the percent and decimal he gets zero points.
6. Roll three dice again and repeat steps 2–4 nine more times.
7. After ten rounds of play, add scores and check scoreboard to see how well you did.

Competition:
If playing against other players, take turns rolling the dice. The first person to get over 700 points is declared the winner.

Sample Game:

Roll one—6, 1, 1 $\frac{1}{1}$ = 100% and 1.00 (Scores 100 points)

Roll two—1, 3, 5 $\frac{3}{5}$ = 60% and .60 (Scores 60 points)

Roll three—2, 3, 6 $\frac{3}{6} = \frac{1}{2}$ = 50% and .50 (Scores 50 points)

Roll four—3, 5, 6 $\frac{5}{6}$ = 83% and .833 (Score 83 points)

Roll five—1, 3, 4 $\frac{3}{4}$ = 75% and .75 (Score 75 points)

Roll six—2, 3, 3 $\frac{3}{3}$ = 100% and 1.00 (Score 100 points)

Roll seven—4, 5, 6 $\frac{5}{6}$ = 83% and .833 (Score 83 points)

Roll eight—3, 4, 5 $\frac{4}{5}$ = 80% and .80 (Score 80 points)

Roll nine—4, 5, 6   Player doesn't know percent and decimal for $\frac{4}{5}$ or $\frac{5}{6}$ (Score 0)

Roll ten—3, 4, 4 $\frac{4}{4}$ = 100% and 1.0 (Score 100 points)

Scoreboard:
A score over 700 is extraordinary!
A score of 699–600 is excellent.
A score of 599–400 is good.
A score of 399–100 is okay.
A score of 99–0 is the pits.

Answer Key:

$\frac{1}{1}, \frac{2}{2}, \frac{3}{3}, \frac{4}{4}, \frac{5}{5}, \frac{6}{6}$ one whole   100%   1.00

$\frac{1}{2}$	one-half	50%	.50		$\frac{2}{3}$	two-thirds	66.6 (67%)	.666
$\frac{1}{3}$	one-third	33.3% (33%)	.333		$\frac{3}{4}$	three-fourths	75%	.75
$\frac{1}{4}$	one-fourth	25%	.25		$\frac{4}{5}$	four-fifths	80%	.80
$\frac{1}{5}$	one-fifth	20%	.20		$\frac{5}{6}$	five-sixths	83.3 (83%)	.833
$\frac{1}{6}$	one-sixth	16.6% (17%)	.166					

What Are the Odds?

Probability

Finding Ratio

Directions

Carefully read each question and decide what is being asked. List the dice combinations and the ratio for each question. Simplify the ratio, if possible.

The Story: When you roll a pair of dice, there are 36 possible combinations. The probability of rolling a pair that totals seven is 6 out of 36 (1,6; 6,1; 2,5; 5,2; 3,4; 4,3) or a ratio of 6:36 (1:6).

1. If you roll a pair of dice, what is the probability of rolling doubles?

2. When rolling one die, what is the probability of getting a six?

3. If you roll a pair of dice, what is the probability that the dots on the dice will total two or twelve?

4. When rolling a pair of dice, the probability of rolling a pair with a total of four, five, nine, or ten is what?

5. When rolling a pair of dice, what is the probability of the dice totaling seven or eleven?

6. When rolling a pair of dice, what is the probability that the dice will total six or less?

7. If you roll a pair of dice and add the numbers indicated by the dots, what are the three totals most likely to come up? What are the ratios?

Deal Me In

Directions

Carefully read each question and decide what is being asked. List the card combinations and the ratio for each question. Reduce the ratio, if possible.

The Story: A deck of playing cards has 52 cards. There are four suits: diamonds (red), hearts (red), clubs (black), and spades (black). There are 13 different kinds of cards: ace, 2, 3, 4, 5, 6, 7, 8, 9, 10, plus three picture cards: jack, queen, king.

1. If you draw a card from the full deck, what are the odds that you will draw a queen?

2. If you draw a card from a full deck, what are the odds that you will draw a red card?

3. The odds of drawing a card with a number from a full deck are what?

4. If you draw a card from a full deck, what are the odds that you will draw a picture card?

5. If you draw a card from a full deck, what are the odds that you will draw a card that isn't a spade?

6. The odds of drawing an ace from a full deck are what?

7. If you shuffle two jokers into a deck of cards and then draw a card, what are the odds of drawing one of the jokers?

The Bookworm Club

Statistics

Mean, Median & Mode

Directions

Finding the *mean* is the same as finding the average. To find the *median*, list the numbers sequentially and find the one that is in the middle. The *mode* is the number that appears most often in the data. Carefully read each question and decide what is being asked. Write any equations needed to solve each problem along with your complete answer.

The Story: The San Gabriel Bookworm Club keeps track of the number of pages members read each day. The table shows the number of pages each member read during a week.

Name	Mon.	Tues.	Wed.	Thurs.	Fri.	Sat.	Sun.
Ethan	190	50	67	96	70	45	91
Jennifer	45	50	66	45	45	100	97
Jacob	63	78	70	88	88	80	60
Madison	66	98	21	57	80	66	66

1. Find the median of pages read by Ethan.

2. The mode of Jennifer's pages read is what?

3. Find the median of pages read by Jacob.

4. What is the mode of Madison's pages read?

5. The mean of Jennifer's pages read is what?

6. On Tuesday, what was the mode of the pages read by all four members?

7. What is the mode of the pages read by Jacob?

Test Scores

Directions

Carefully read each question and decide what is being asked. Write the equations needed to solve each problem along with your complete answer.

The Story: Mr. Roake keeps track of students' average test scores by averaging percents in each subject. Use the table below to answer the questions.

Name	Reading	Math	Spelling	Science	Social Studies
Nicole	88%	90%	92%	86%	99%
Jasmine	99%	99%	99%	82%	70%
Anna	99%	88%	96%	89%	95%
Isaiah	97%	98%	98%	79%	98%
Cameron	88%	92%	99%	95%	94%
Justin	99%	98%	92%	92%	90%

1. Find the median of Nicole's test averages in all five subjects.

2. What is the mode of Jasmine's test averages for all five subjects?

5. Find the mean for the social studies test averages.

3.. In all five subjects, Anna's median test average is what?

6. The mean score for spelling test averages is what?

4. What is the mode of Isaiah's test averages in all five subjects?

7. Which student has a median test average of 92% for all five subjects?

Name _____ Date _____

All Dressed Up

Logic

Problem Solving

Directions

Carefully read each clue and decide what is being said. On the chart, record the information given in each clue. To find the answers, check to see what possibilities are left.

The Story: Four women, Mrs. Brown, Mrs. Green, Mrs. White, and Mrs. Black each bought a new dress. One of the new dresses is brown, one is green, one is white, and one is black.

	brown	green	white	black
Mrs. Brown				
Mrs. Green				
Mrs. White				
Mrs. Black				

Clues

1. Only one woman is wearing the same color dress as her name.

2. Mrs. Green is wearing the black or white dress.

3. Mrs. Brown is wearing the green or white dress.

4. Mrs. Black is wearing the brown or black dress.

5. Mrs. White is wearing the brown or green dress.

6. Mrs. Green is not wearing the black dress.

Answers

Which woman is wearing which dress?

brown dress: _____

green dress: _____

white dress: _____

black dress: _____

Hungry Boys

Logic

Problem Solving

Directions

Carefully read each clue and decide what is being said. On the chart, record the information given in each clue. To find the answers, check to see what possibilities are left.

The Story: Five boys went to lunch: Tyler, Darius, Joseph, Andrew, and Chiyong. One boy had pepperoni pizza, one had a hot dog, one had a hamburger, one had a salad, and one had fish 'n' chips.

	pizza	hot dog	hamburger	salad	fish 'n' chips
Tyler					
Darius					
Joseph					
Andrew					
Chiyong					

Clues

1. Tyler had a hot dog or a salad.

2. Joseph had pepperoni pizza or a hot dog.

3. Chiyong didn't have pepperoni pizza or a hot dog.

4. Andrew had a salad or fish and chips.

5. Darius is vegetarian.

Answers

Which boy ate which lunch?

pizza: _____

hot dog: _____

hamburger: _____

salad: _____

fish 'n' chips: _____

What Kind of Pet?

Directions

Carefully read each clue and decide what is being said. On the chart, record the information given in each clue. To find the answers, check to see what possibilities are left.

The Story: Five children have pets including birds, fish, horses, dogs, and cats. Each child has only one kind of pet but some have more than one of that kind of pet. Each child has a different kind of pet from the other children. Two children have 1 pet; 1 child has 2 pets, 1 child has 3 pets, and 1 child has 5 pets.

	dog(s)	cat(s)	horse(s)	fish	bird(s)	1	1	2	3	5
Becky										
James										
Alonzo										
Cherise										
Terrel										

Clues

1. Becky has two pets, and they aren't dogs or fish.

2. Terrel has more than two pets, and they aren't horses or fish.

3. James has only one pet, and it's a dog or cat.

4. Cherise has only one pet, and it isn't a bird or cat.

5. Alonzo doesn't have the most pets but he has more than Becky.

6. Terrel keeps his pets in a cage.

7. Alonzo can ride one of his pets in a parade.

Answers

How many and what kind of pet does each child have?

Becky: _____

James: _____

Alonzo: _____

Cherise: _____

Terrel: _____

Make a Mean, Median, or Mode

Statistics

Culminating Game

Object of the Game:
Get as many points as possible by figuring the mean, median, or mode of the five dice.

Directions:
1. Number a sheet of paper from one to five.
2. Roll five dice.
3. Begin by figuring the mean of the five numbers indicated by the dice. If there is a remainder, the score is 0.
4. Next, figure the median and add the points to the mean.
5. Finally, look for a mode and add the points to the total. If there is no mode, the score is 0.
6. The total points for mean, median, and mode equal the player's score for that round.
7. Repeat for four more rounds. Add scores and check the scoreboard to see how well you did.

Competition:
Take turns. The first to get 50 points is the winner.

Materials Needed:
Paper, pencil, five dice

Scoreboard:
A score over 50 is extraordinary!
A score of 49–40 is excellent.
A score of 39–20 is good.
A score of 19–10 is okay.
A score of 9–0 is the pits.

Sample Game:
Roll one—6, 5, 5, 1, 1   (Score is 5 points for this round.)
Mean: $6 + 5 + 5 + 1 + 1 = 18/5 = 3 \text{ R } 3$ (Scores 0 points for mean.)
Median: Five is the median   (Score 5 points for median.)
Mode: No mode   (Score 0 points for mode.)
Roll two—1, 3, 5, 5, 6   (Score is 14 points for this round. Game total is 19.)
Mean: $1 + 3 + 5 + 5 + 6 = 20/5 = 4$ (Score 4 points for mean.)
Median: Five is the median   (Score 5 points for median.)
Mode: Five is the mode   (Score 5 points for mode.)
Roll three—1, 2, 2, 3, 6   (Score 4 points for this round. Game total is 23.)
Mean: $1 + 2 + 2 + 3 + 6 = 14/5 = 2 \text{ R } 4$ (Score 0 points for mean.)
Median: Two is the median   (Score 2 points for median.)
Mode: Two is the mode   (Score 2 points for mode.)
Roll four—2, 2, 4, 6, 6   (Score 8 points for this round. Game total is 31.)
Mean: $2 + 2 + 4 + 6 + 6 = 20/5 = 4$ (Score 4 points for mean.)
Median: Four is the median   (Score 4 points for median.)
Mode: No mode   (Score 0 points for mode.)
Roll five—2, 3, 4, 4, 5   (Score 8 points for this round. Game total is 39.)
Mean: $2 + 3 + 4 + 4 + 5 = 18/5 = 3 \text{ R } 3$ (Score 0 points for mean.)
Median: Four is the median   (Score 4 points for median.)
Mode: Four is the mode   (Score 4 points for mode.)

Post Test

The Story

Animals vary in their speeds. Chickens can run 9 mph, domestic pigs can run 11 mph, squirrels can run 12 mph, a black mamba snake can travel 20 mph, a pet cat can run 30 mph, and a giraffe can run 32 mph.

1. If a chicken could maintain its fastest speed, how far could it run in six hours?

   a. 36 miles   b. 54 miles
   c. 90 miles   d. 600 miles

2. If all of the animals were on a relay team and each ran for an hour, altogether, how far would they travel?

3. In half an hour, how much farther can a cat travel than a squirrel?

4. The average speed of the animals is

   a. 10 mph   b. 12 mph
   c. 16 mph   d. 19 mph

5. A mamba snake can travel as far in three hours as a cat can run in two hours. True or false?

The Story

Grace baked a huge chocolate sheet cake and cut it into 20 pieces.

6. What fractional part of the cake is represented by five pieces?

   a. $\frac{1}{5}$ b. $\frac{1}{2}$
   c. $\frac{1}{4}$ d. $\frac{1}{10}$

7. Ten pieces of cake represents 50% of the whole cake. True or false?

8. What decimal does six pieces of the cake represent?

   a. 0.6   b. 0.3
   c. 0.10   d. 3.33

9. Four tenths of the cake is how many pieces of cake?

10. If Grace served 17 pieces of her cake, what fractional part of the cake is left?

Post Test

The Story

For her birthday party, Mackenzie baked two pies, cherry and apple. She cut the cherry pie into eight pieces. She cut the apple pie into six pieces.

cherry   apple

11. What fraction represents six pieces of the cherry pie?

   a. $\frac{1}{8}$ b. $\frac{1}{4}$

   c. $\frac{1}{2}$ d. $\frac{3}{4}$

12. If Julia ate half of an apple pie, she ate $\frac{2}{6}$ of the pie. True or false?

13. If MacKenzie bakes two cherry pies, cuts them the same way, and sells each piece for 50¢, how much money can she make in all?

   a. $4.00   b. $6.00
   c. $8.00   d. $16.00

14. What decimal is represented by two pieces of apple pie?

15. What fractional part of a whole pie is represented by two pieces of cherry pie and three pieces of apple pie?

The Story

Coach David kept track of the points made by the first-string basketball players in the first five games. Brandon scored 1, 8, 3, 0, and 8 points. Zach scored 8, 4, 4, 4, and 6 points. Tony scored 8, 10, 6, 2, and 4 points. Chris scored 4, 6, 6, 12, and 10 points. Darrel scored 8, 12, 10, 8, and 12 points.

16. The mean score for Brandon's games is

   a. 4 points   b. 8 points
   c. 5 points   d. 2 points

17. What is the mode of Zach's scores?

18. Tony has a median score of six. True or false?

19. The mode score for the first game was

   a. 9 points   b. 8 points
   c. 6 points   d. 2 points

20. What is the median of Chris's scores?

Answer Key

Page 5
1. $41 + 20 + 15 + 15 = 91$ yr.
2. $30 + 27 + 20 + 6 = 83$ yr.
3. $15 + 15 + 12 + 10 = 52$ yr.
4. $30 + 50 + 27 + 6 = 113$ yr.
5. $15 + 15 + 10 + 3 = 43$ yr.
6. $3 + 10 + 15 + 12 = 40$ yr.
7. $50 + 77 + 54 + 50 + 50 = 281$ yr.

Page 6
1. $538 + 506 = 1,044$ mi.
2. $498 + 465 = 963$ mi.
3. $521 + 512 + 503 = 1,536$ mi.
4. $535 + 498 + 526 = 1,559$ mi.
5. $496 + 465 + 487 = 1,448$ mi.
6. $523 + 503 + 468 = 1,494$ mi.
7. $490 + 524 + 526 = 1,540$ mi.

Page 7
1. $93 - 28 = 65$ books
2. $81 - 56 = 25$ books
3. $78 - 59 = 19$ books
4. $63 - 58 = 5$ books
5. $67 - 58 = 9$ books
6. $91 - 79 = 12$ books
7. $41 - 35 = 6$ books

Page 8
1. $1879 - 1851 = 28$ years
2. $1817 - 1783 = 34$ years
3. $1970 - 105 = 1,865$ years
4. $1903 - 1785 = 118$ years
5. $1937 - 1888 = 49$ years
6. $1888 - 1642 = 246$ years
7. $1927 - 1885 = 42$ years

Page 9
1. $12 + 10 + 24 + 8 + 8 = 62$; $12 + 12 + 6 + 20 + 8 = 58$; $62 > 58$; brownies
2. $12 + 24 + 30 + 36 + 36 = 138$; $12 + 8 + 12 + 6 + 0 = 38$; $138 - 38 = 100$ cookies
3. $12 + 12 + 6 + 20 + 8 = 58$; $12 + 24 + 30 + 36 + 36 = 138$; $138 > 58$; cookies
4. $10 + 12 + 24 + 8 = 54$; $12 + 12 + 12 + 12 = 48$; $54 - 48 = 6$ desserts
5. $24 + 6 + 30 + 12 = 72$; $8 + 20 + 36 + 6 = 70$; $72 - 70 = 2$ desserts
6. $10 + 12 + 24 + 8 = 54$; $72 - 54 = 18$ desserts
7. $8 + 8 + 36 + 0 = 52$; $72 - 52 = 20$ desserts

Page 10
(T: 362, 365, 312, 349, 371, 397)
1. $365 - 364 = 1$ point
2. $97 + 93 = 190$; $90 + 91 = 181$; $190 - 181 = 9$ points
3. $99 + 100 = 199$; $100 + 98 = 198$; $199 - 198 = 1$ point
4. $397 - 371 = 26$ points
5. $364 - 312 = 52$ points
6. $349 - 312 = 37$ points
7. $371 - 365 = 6$ points

Page 11
1. $68 \times 3 = \$204,000,000$
2. $57 \times 3 = \$171,000,000$
3. $40 \times 8 = \$320,000,000$
4. $67 \times 6 = \$402,000,000$
5. $50 \times 4 = \$200,000,000$
6. $38 \times 8 = \$304,000,000$
7. $35 \times 3 = \$105,000,000$

Page 12
1. $610 \times 12 = 7,320$; $510 \times 12 = 6,120$; $7,320 + 6,120 = 13,440$ newspapers
2. $521 \times 5 = 2,605$; $713 \times 5 = 3,565$; $2,605 + 3,565 = 6,170$ bottles
3. $677 \times 15 = 10,155$; $589 \times 15 = 8,835$; $10,155 + 8,835 = 18,990$ boxes
4. $622 \times 15 = 9,330$; $521 \times 15 = 7,815$; $713 \times 15 = 10,695$; $,330 + 7,815 + 10,695 = 27,840$ bottles
5. $610 \times 17 = 10,370$; $510 \times 17 = 8,670$; $701 \times 17 = 11,917$; $10,370 + 8,670 + 11,917 = 30,957$ newspapers
6. $510 \times 18 = 9,180$; $701 \times 18 = 12,618$; $9,180 + 12,618 = 21,798$ newspapers
7. $610 + 510 + 701 = 1,821$; $1,821 \times 5 = 9,105$; $622 + 521 + 713 = 1,856$; $1,856 \times 5 = 9,280$; $589 + 489 + 677 = 1,755$; $1,755 \times 5 = 8,776$; $9,105 + 9,280 + 8,775 = 27,160$ cents ($\$271.60$)

Page 13
1. $702 \div 8 = 87$ cards; yes
2. $616 \div 7 = 88$; yes
3. $546 \div 8 = 68$ cards, R2
4. $699 \div 6 = 116$ R3; 117 pg.
5. $293 \div 4 = 73$ R1; 1 wall
6. $508 \div 9 = 56$ cards, R4
7. $846 \div 9 = 94$ cards, R0

Page 14
1. $\$132 \div 44 = \$3$
2. $\$365 \div 73 = \$5$
3. $\$336 \div 84 = \$4$
4. $\$536 \div 67 = \$8$
5. $\$637 \div 91 = \$7$
6. $\$330 \div 55 = \$6$
7. $\$828 \div 92 = \$9$

Page 15
1. $80 + 90 = 170$ pages
2. $220 - 180 = 40$ pages
3. $120 \times 0 = 0$
4. $120 \div 4 = 30$ pages
5. $150 \div 5 = 30$ pages
6. $144 + 0 + 99 + 0 = 243$ pg.
7. $144 + 67 + 99 + 10 + 150 = 470$; $470 \div 5 = 94$ pg.

Page 16
1. $111 \times 6 = 666$; $45 \times 6 = 270$; $666 - 270 = 396$ papers
2. $1,332 \div 666 = 2$ weeks
3. $59 \times 6 = 354$; $45 \times 6 = 270$; $354 - 270 = 84$ papers
4. $1,770 \div 354 = 5$ weeks
5. $111 \times 6 = 666$; $59 \times 6 = 354$; $666 - 354 = 312$ papers
6. $540 \div 45 = 12$; $12 \div 6 = 2$ wk.
7. $111 \times 6 = 666$; $59 \times 6 = 354$; $45 \times 6 = 270$; $666 + 354 + 270 = 1,290$ papers

Page 17
1. $30 \times 5 = 150$; $15 \times 5 = 75$; $75 + 60 = 135$; $150 - 135 = 15$ min.
2. $20 \times 7 = 140$; $15 \times 5 = 75$; $75 + 60 = 135$; $140 - 135 = 5$ min.
3. $30 \times 5 = 150$; $60 \times 5 = 300$; $300 \div 150 = 2$ weeks
4. $5 \times 15 = 75$; $75 + 60 = 135$; $135 \times 4 = 540$ min.
5. $30 \times 5 = 150$; $150 \times 50 = 7,500$; $7,500 \div 60 = 125$ hr.
6. $30 \times 5 = 150$; $20 \times 7 = 140$; $150 - 140 = 10$; $10 \times 4 = 40$ min.
7. $30 \times 5 = 150$; $20 \times 7 = 140$; $15 \times 5 = 75 + 60 = 135$; $150 + 140 + 135 = 425$; $425 \div 60 = 7$ R5; less

Page 19
1. $10.8 + 13.6 = 24.4\%$
2. $29.2 + 45.6 = 74.8\%$
3. $44.8 + 9.4 = 54.2\%$
4. $44.5 + 9.2 + 13.4 = 67.1\%$
5. $33.0 + 44.9 + 8.2 + 13.9 = 100\%$
6. $29.2 + 13.5 = 42.7\%$
7. $44.9 + 8.2 + 13.9 = 67\%$; 1991

Page 20
1. $49.6 - 48.12 = 1.48$ sec.
2. $50.1 - 49.3 = 0.8$ sec.
3. $50.1 - 47.54 = 2.56$ sec.
4. $47.75 - 47.64 = 0.11$ sec.
5. $48.7 - 48.12 = 0.58$ sec.
6. $47.19 - 46.78 = 0.41$ sec.
7. $47.82 - 47.19 = 0.63$ sec.

Page 21
1. $20.4 \times 2 = 40.8$ km
2. $18.5 \times 2 = 37$; $37 \times 5 = 185$ km
3. $9.3 \times 2 = 18.6$; $18.6 \times 30 = 558$ km
4. $2.3 \times 2 = 4.6$; $4.6 \times 20 = 92$ km
5. $6.7 \times 2 = 13.4$; $13.4 \times 12 = 160.8$ km
6. $9.3 \times 2 = 18.6$; $18.6 \times 35 = 651$ km
7. $20.4 \times 2 = 40.8$; $40.8 \times 5 = 204$; $204 > 200$; more

Page 22
1. $49.50 - 40.25 = 9.25$ mph
2. $.03 \times 2 = .06$; $.03 \times 4 = .12$; $.06 + .12 = .18$ mi.
3. $25.3 \times 4 = 101.2$ miles
4. $100 \times .03 = 3$ miles
5. $40.25 \times 5 = 201.25$ mi.
6. $25.30 - .03 = 25.27$ mph
7. $.03 \times 24 = 0.72$; $0.72 \times 7 = 5.04$; $5.04 \times 5 = 25.20$; $25.20 < 25.30$; no

Page 23
1. $\$6.25 + 2.15 + 1.55 + 0.50 = \$10.45$
2. $\$7.00 - 4.25 = \$2.75$
3. $\$7.00 \times 5 = \$35.00$; $5 \times \$0.50 = \$2.50$; $\$35.00 + 2.50 = \$37.50$
4. $\$7.75 - 6.00 = \$1.75$
5. $\$3.50 \times 20 = \$70.00$
6. $\$0.75 \times 6 = \$4.50$; $\$4.50 + 2.85 = \$7.35$
7. $8 \times \$7.75 = \$62.00$; $8 \times \$0.90 = \$7.20$; $\$62.00 + 7.20 = \$69.20$

Page 24
1. $40\% + 10\% = 50\%$
2. $50\% + 20\% = 70\%$
3. $20\% + 0\% = 20\%$
4. $40\% + 30\% = 70\%$
5. $40\% - 30\% = 10\%$
6. $100\% - 90\% = 10\%$
7. $50\% - 30\% = 20\%$

Answer Key

Page 25
1. 5% x 6 = 30%
2. 85% − 70% = 15%
3. 5% x 9 = 45%
4. 100% − 0% = 100%
5. 5% x 6 = 30%; 5% x 9 = 45%; 30% + 45% = 75%
6. 1 x 5% = 5%; 100% − 5% = 95%; A
7. 5% x 18 = 90%; 5% x 11 = 55%; 90% − 55% = 35%

Page 26
1. 15% + 15% = 30%
2. 10% + 5% + 20% = 35%
3. 15% − 10% = 5%
4. 100% − 15% = 85%
5. 20% + 15% +5% = 40%
6. 15% + 5% = 20%; 100% − 20% = 80%
7. 30% (.30) x 20 = 6 students

Page 27
1. $\frac{10}{32} + \frac{9}{32} = \frac{19}{32}$; $\frac{3}{32} + \frac{2}{32} = \frac{5}{32}$ $\frac{19}{32} - \frac{5}{32} = \frac{14}{32} (\frac{7}{16})$ of students
2. $\frac{10}{32} + \frac{7}{32} = \frac{17}{32}$; $\frac{3}{32} + \frac{1}{32} = \frac{4}{32}$ $\frac{17}{32} - \frac{4}{32} = \frac{13}{32}$ of students
3. $\frac{7}{32} + \frac{3}{32} + \frac{1}{32} = \frac{11}{32}$; $\frac{11}{32} > \frac{10}{32}$; chicken, shrimp, or hot dogs
4. $\frac{9}{32} + \frac{3}{32} = \frac{12}{32}$; $\frac{1}{32} + \frac{10}{32} = \frac{11}{32}$; $\frac{12}{32} > \frac{11}{32}$; burgers or shrimp
5. $\frac{1}{16} = \frac{2}{32}$; steaks
6. $\frac{9}{32} + \frac{7}{32} + \frac{3}{32} = \frac{19}{32}$ of the class
7. $\frac{3}{32} + \frac{2}{32} = \frac{5}{32}$; $\frac{7}{32} > \frac{5}{32}$; chicken

Page 28
1. $\frac{5}{30} + \frac{4}{30} = \frac{9}{30} (\frac{3}{10})$ of the days
2. $\frac{4}{30} + \frac{4}{30} = \frac{8}{30} (\frac{4}{15})$ of the days
3. $\frac{30}{30} - \frac{12}{30} = \frac{18}{30} (\frac{9}{15})$ of the dates
4. $\frac{4}{30} + \frac{4}{30} + \frac{5}{30} = \frac{13}{30}$ of the days
5. $\frac{5}{30} + \frac{4}{30} = \frac{9}{30} (\frac{3}{10})$
6. $\frac{4}{30} + \frac{4}{30} + \frac{4}{30} = \frac{12}{30} (\frac{2}{5})$ of the days
7. $\frac{5}{30} - \frac{4}{30} = \frac{1}{30}$

Page 29
1. $\frac{9}{12} < \frac{10}{12}$; $\frac{3}{4} < \frac{5}{6}$; $\frac{5}{6}$ meter
2. $\frac{9}{12} > \frac{8}{12}$; $\frac{9}{12} > \frac{4}{6}$
3. $\frac{4}{12} > \frac{3}{12}$; $\frac{1}{4} > \frac{1}{3}$; $\frac{1}{3}$ meter
4. $\frac{3}{6} > \frac{2}{6}$; $\frac{1}{2} > \frac{1}{3}$
5. $\frac{9}{12} = \frac{9}{12}$; $\frac{9}{12} = \frac{3}{4}$
6. $\frac{10}{12} + \frac{1}{12} = \frac{11}{12}$; $\frac{11}{12} < \frac{12}{12}$; less
7. $\frac{22}{24} > \frac{21}{24}$; $\frac{11}{12} > \frac{7}{8}$; $\frac{11}{12}$ meter

Page 30
1. $\frac{3}{24} < \frac{4}{24}$; $\frac{1}{8} < \frac{1}{6}$; Sophia
2. $\frac{12}{24} < \frac{15}{24}$; $\frac{3}{6} < \frac{5}{8}$; Spike
3. $\frac{9}{24} > \frac{8}{24}$; $\frac{3}{8} > \frac{2}{6}$; Jolie
4. $\frac{1}{2} = \frac{1}{2}$; $\frac{4}{8} = \frac{3}{6}$; neither
5. $\frac{8}{8} - \frac{1}{8} = \frac{7}{8}$; $\frac{6}{6} - \frac{2}{6} = \frac{4}{6}$; $\frac{21}{24} > \frac{16}{24}$; $\frac{7}{8} > \frac{4}{6}$; cherry cheesecake
6. $\frac{8}{8} - \frac{1}{2} = \frac{4}{8}$; $\frac{6}{6} - \frac{2}{3} = \frac{2}{6}$; $\frac{4}{8} > \frac{2}{6}$; cheesecake
7. $\frac{12}{24} < \frac{16}{24}$; $\frac{4}{8} < \frac{4}{6}$; peach cobbler

Page 31
1. $\frac{4}{6} + \frac{2}{6} = \frac{20}{24} (\frac{5}{6})$ of a yard
2. $\frac{3}{4} + \frac{1}{3} = \frac{13}{12} (1\frac{1}{12})$ yards
3. $\frac{1}{2} + \frac{1}{3} = \frac{5}{6}$ of a yard
4. $\frac{3}{6} = \frac{4}{8} (= \frac{1}{2})$; neither
5. $1 = \frac{8}{8}$; 8 hankies
6. $\frac{1}{2} < \frac{4}{6}$; no

Page 32
1. $\frac{16}{16} - \frac{5}{16} = \frac{11}{16}$ of the cake
2. $\frac{1}{2} + \frac{2}{4} = \frac{4}{4}$ (1) cake
3. $\frac{1}{4} + \frac{4}{16} = \frac{8}{16} (\frac{1}{2})$ of a cake
4. $\frac{4}{16} = \frac{1}{4}$ of the cake
5. $\frac{1}{2} + \frac{3}{16} = \frac{11}{16}$ of a cake
6. $\frac{1}{2} + \frac{1}{4} + \frac{1}{16} = \frac{13}{16}$ of a cake
7. $\frac{1}{2} = \frac{8}{16}$; 8 pieces

Page 33
1. 5 x 2 = 10; $\frac{16}{16} - \frac{10}{16} = \frac{6}{16} (\frac{3}{8})$ of the peanut cluster bar
2. $\frac{3}{2} = 1\frac{1}{2}$ dark chocolate bars
3. $\frac{16}{16} \div 4 = \frac{16}{64} (\frac{4}{16})$; 4 chunks
4. $\frac{4}{8} = \frac{2}{4}$; 4 triangles
5. $\frac{16}{16} - \frac{7}{16} = \frac{9}{16}$ of the peanut cluster bar
6. $\frac{12}{16} = \frac{6}{8}$; 12 peanut cluster chunks
7. $\frac{1}{2} = \frac{8}{16}$; 8 peanut cluster chunks

Page 34
1. 6 x $\frac{1}{20} = \frac{6}{20} (\frac{3}{10})$ of the whole
2. 8 x .05 = .40
3. 10 x 5% = 50%
4. 12 x $\frac{1}{20} = \frac{12}{20} (\frac{3}{5})$ of the whole
5. .35 ÷ .05 = 7 sections
6. 45% ÷ 5% = 9 sections
7. 50% ÷ 5% = 10 sections; 10 x $\frac{1}{20} = \frac{10}{20} (\frac{1}{2})$ of the wheel

Page 35
1. 50% = .50
2. $\frac{8}{100}$ = 8%
3. $\frac{80}{100}$ = 80%
4. $\frac{35}{100}$ = .35
5. .75 = $\frac{75}{100}$
6. .10 = 10%

Page 37
1. (1,1; 2,2; 3,3; 4,4; 5,5; 6,6); 6:36 (1:6)
2. 1:6
3. (1,1; 6,6); 2:36 (1:18)
4. (2,2; 1,3; 2,3; 1,4; 3,6; 4,5; 5,5; 4,6; 3,1; 3,2; 4,1; 6,3; 5,4; 6,4); 14:36 (7:18)
5. (1,6; 6,1; 2,5; 5,2; 3,4; 4,3; 5,6; 6,5); 8:36 (2:9)
6. (1,1; 1,2; 2,1; 1,3; 3,1; 1,4; 4,1; 4,2; 5,1; 1,5; 2,2; 2,3; 2,4; 3,2; 3,3); 15:36
7. 7—6:36 (1:6); 8—5:36; 6—5:36

Page 38
1. (Q of D, Q of H, Q of C, Q of S); 4:52 (1:13)
2. 13 + 13 = 26; 26:52 (1:2)
3. (2, 3, 4, 5, 6, 7, 8, 9, 10 of four suits); 9 x 4 = 36; 36:52 (9:13)
4. (J, Q, K of four suits); 3 x 4 = 12; 12:52 (3:13)
5. 13 x 3 = 39; 39:52
6. (A of D, A of H, A of C, A of S); 4:52 (1:13)
7. 52 + 2 = 54; 2:54 (1: 27)

Page 39
1. 70
2. 45
3. 78
4. 66
5. 45 + 50 + 66 + 45 + 45 + 100 + 97 = 448; 448 ÷ 7 = 64 pages
6. 50
7. 88

Page 40
1. 90%
2. 99%
3. 95%
4. 98%
5. 99% + 70% + 95% + 98% + 94% + 90% = 546; 546 ÷ 6 = 91%
6. 92% + 99% + 96% + 98% + 99% + 92% = 576; 576 ÷ 6 = 96%
7. Justin

Page 41
brown dress: Mrs. White
green dress: Mrs. Brown
white dress: Mrs. Green
black dress: Mrs. Black

Page 42
pizza: Joseph
hot dog: Tyler
hamburger: Chiyong
salad: Darius
fish 'n' chips: Andrew

Page 43
Becky: 2 cats
James: 1 dog
Alonzo: 3 horses
Cherise: 1 fish
Terrel: 5 birds

Page 45
1. b. 54 miles
2. 114 miles
3. 9 miles
4. d. 19 mph
5. true
6. c. 1/4
7. true
8. b. 0.3
9. 8 pieces
10. $\frac{3}{20}$ of the cake

Page 46
11. d. 3/4
12. false
13. c. $8.00
14. .33
15. $\frac{18}{24} (\frac{3}{4})$ of a pie
16. a. 4 points
17. 4 points
18. true
19. b. 8
20. 6 points